JUNIOR ROOM
PUBLIC LIBRARY
Stoneham, Mass.

U.S. WARS

THE REVOLUTIONARY WAR

A MyReportLinks.com Book

Carl R. Green

MyReportLinks.com Books
an imprint of
 Enslow Publishers, Inc.
Box 398, 40 Industrial Road
Berkeley Heights, NJ 07922
USA

MyReportLinks.com Books, an imprint of Enslow Publishers, Inc.

Copyright © 2002 by Enslow Publishers, Inc.

All rights reserved.

No part of this book may be reproduced by any means
without the written permission of the publisher.

Library of Congress Cataloging-in-Publication Data

Green, Carl R.
    The Revolutionary War / Carl R. Green.
        p. cm.—(U.S. wars)
    Includes bibliographical references and index.
    Summary: Discusses the military tactics, battles, and famous figures of
the war that gained the American colonies their independence from Great
Britain. Includes Internet links to Web sites, source documents, and
illustrations related to the war.
    ISBN 0-7660-5089-0
    1. United States—History—Revolution, 1775–1783—Juvenile literature.
[1. United States—History—Revolution, 1775–1783.] I. Title. II. Series.
E208 .G74 2002
973.3—dc21
                                    2001008193

Printed in the United States of America

10 9 8 7 6 5 4 3 2 1

To Our Readers:
Through the purchase of this book, you and your library gain access to the Report Links that specifically
back up this book.
The Publisher will provide access to the Report Links that back up this book and will keep these Report
Links up to date on **www.myreportlinks.com** for three years from the book's first publication date.
We have done our best to make sure all Internet addresses in this book were active and appropriate when we
went to press. However, the author and the Publisher have no control over, and assume no liability for, the
material available on those Internet sites or on other Web sites they may link to.
The usage of the MyReportLinks.com Books Web site is subject to the terms and conditions stated on the
Usage Policy Statement on **www.myreportlinks.com**.
In the future, a password may be required to access the Report Links that back up this book. The password
is found on the bottom of page 4 of this book.
Any comments or suggestions can be sent by e-mail to comments@myreportlinks.com or to the address on
the back cover.

Photo Credits: © Corel Corporation, pp. 1 (background), 3; Courtesy of America's Story from America's
Library, p. 30; Courtesy of MyReportLinks.com Books, p. 4; Courtesy of PBS: Perspectives on Liberty,
p. 19; Courtesy of Spy Letters of the American Revolution: From the Collection of the Clements Library, pp.
22, 29; Courtesy of The History Place, pp. 13, 18, 21, 34; Courtesy of the State Department, p. 39; Courtesy
of United States Military Academy, p. 27; Enslow Publishers, Inc., pp. 15, 40; Library of Congress, pp. 17,
20; National Archives, pp. 11, 25, 32, 37, 42; Painting by Don Troiani, www.historicalprints.com, p. 1.

Cover Photo: Painting by Don Troiani, www.historicalprints.com

Cover Description: The Battle of Cowpens

Contents

MyReportLinks.com Books
Great Books, Great Links, Great for Research!

MyReportLinks.com Books present the information you need to learn about your report subject. In addition, they show you where to go on the Internet for more information. The pre-evaluated Report Links that back up this book are kept up to date on **www.myreportlinks.com**. With the purchase of a MyReportLinks.com Books title, you and your library gain access to the Report Links that specifically back up that book. The Report Links save hours of research time and link to dozens—even hundreds—of Web sites, source documents, and photos related to your report topic.

Please see "To Our Readers" on the Copyright page for important information about this book, the MyReportLinks.com Books Web site, and the Report Links that back up this book.

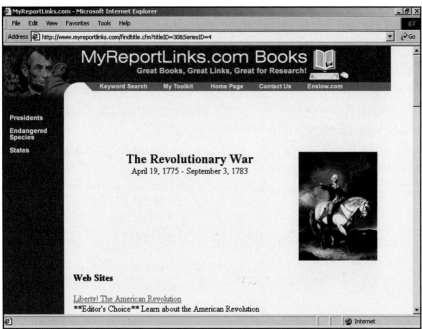

Access:

The Publisher will provide access to the Report Links that back up this book and will try to keep these Report Links up to date on our Web site for three years from the book's first publication date. Please enter **AAR1378** if asked for a password.

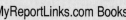
Report Links

The Internet sites described below can be accessed at
http://www.myreportlinks.com

*Editor's choice

▶ **Liberty! The American Revolution**
This PBS Web site provides an online companion to "LIBERTY! The American Revolution." This Web site features images, time lines, war highlights, a game, and much more.

Link to this Internet site from http://www.myreportlinks.com

*Editor's choice

▶ **Maps of the American Revolution**
Revisit the sites of the American Revolution through this collection of maps from the United States Military Academy. Several of the maps show troop movements in key battles.

Link to this Internet site from http://www.myreportlinks.com

*Editor's choice

▶ **Drums Along the Mohawk**
At this Web site you can explore New York's Mohawk Valley during the years of the Revolutionary War. Here you will find a comprehensive history about the war as it pertained to New York. You will also find profiles of patriots and loyalists.

Link to this Internet site from http://www.myreportlinks.com

*Editor's choice

▶ **Historic Valley Forge**
Read the story of the encampment of the Continental Army at Valley Forge in southeastern Pennsylvania. You will also learn how the troops who arrived in December 1777 were transformed into proud and confident soldiers by the time they departed in late June 1778.

Link to this Internet site from http://www.myreportlinks.com

*Editor's choice

▶ **Spy Letters of the American Revolution**
This site contains fascinating stories of espionage during the Revolutionary War. Among the famous spies covered here are John Andre and Benedict Arnold.

Link to this Internet site from http://www.myreportlinks.com

*Editor's choice

▶ **The Battle of Saratoga**
At this Web site you can explore the Battle of Saratoga. Here you will learn about the British and American troops, the history of the battle, and find a gallery of images.

Link to this Internet site from http://www.myreportlinks.com

Report Links

➤ The Internet sites described below can be accessed at
http://www.myreportlinks.com

▶ **African American Freedom Fighters: Soldiers for Liberty**

At this Web site you will learn about African Americans who fought in
United States wars over the years. Included is a section covering the
Revolutionary War.

Link to this Internet site from http://www.myreportlinks.com

▶ **America's Freedom Documents**

The principles for which the founding fathers fought in the American
Revolution are described in the documents found at this site. Included are the
Declaration of Independence, the Constitution, and the Bill of Rights.

Link to this Internet site from http://www.myreportlinks.com

▶ **American Independence Museum**

From the American Independence Museum in Exeter, New Hampshire, comes
this overview of the war as it affected a typical New England village. Here you
can visit Exeter's Ladd-Gilman House and the Folsom Tavern.

Link to this Internet site from http://www.myreportlinks.com

▶ **American Military History**

The United States Army provides an online version of American Military
History. Here you will find a chapter on the American Revolution, and
other wars.

Link to this Internet site from http://www.myreportlinks.com

▶ **The American Revolution**

At this Web site you will find a collection of essays written by scholars about
the Revolutionary War. You will also find links to more resources on the war.

Link to this Internet site from http://www.myreportlinks.com

▶ **The American Revolution**

At this Web site you will find numerous links to information about
the Revolutionary War, including scholarly writings, flags, reenactments,
and more.

Link to this Internet site from http://www.myreportlinks.com

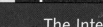

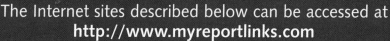

The Internet sites described below can be accessed at
http://www.myreportlinks.com

▶**The American Revolution and Its Era: Maps and Charts of North America and the West Indies, 1750–1789**
This Library of Congress site contains maps and marine charts from the period of the Revolutionary War.

Link to this Internet site from http://www.myreportlinks.com

▶**The American Revolution: The Struggle for Independence**
At this Web site you will find a wealth of information about the American Revolution, including articles, biographies, and weapons of war.

Link to this Internet site from http://www.myreportlinks.com

▶**The Boston Tea Party**
Learn about some of the events leading up to the Boston Tea Party and how the Sons of Liberty took over the ships in the Boston Harbor.

Link to this Internet site from http://www.myreportlinks.com

▶**The Colonies during the Revolutionary War**
At this Web site you will find an interactive map of the main battles of the Revolutionary War. Each battle site is complete with a description of the battle and images showing the battlefield and the soldiers.

Link to this Internet site from http://www.myreportlinks.com

▶**The Colored Patriots of the American Revolution**
The site features the text of a lengthy report that celebrates the contributions of African Americans to the cause of liberty during the Revolutionary War. Here you will find the stories of Crispus Attucks, Henry Boyd, Lewis Hayden, and others.

Link to this Internet site from http://www.myreportlinks.com

▶**Fact Monster: American Revolution**
At this Web site, you will get the basic facts about the Revolutionary War from the Fact Monster. You will learn about the causes and outcome of the Revolutionary War, as well as key figures and events of the period.

Link to this Internet site from http://www.myreportlinks.com

 The Internet sites described below can be accessed at
http://www.myreportlinks.com

▶**Frontier Forts in the American Revolution**
Visit this site to learn about the important role frontier forts played in the
American Revolution. These forts offered American colonists refuge from
British forces or American Indian war parties.

Link to this Internet site from http://www.myreportlinks.com

▶**Historic Documents of the United States**
This Web site holds a collection of historic documents relating to the events
leading up to the Revolutionary War.

Link to this Internet site from http://www.myreportlinks.com

▶**The History Place: American Revolution**
This time line chronicles America's march towards independence, from the
earliest explorations of North America through 1790. Entries are detailed,
and provide an excellent quick reference guide to this critical period in
American history.

Link to this Internet site from http://www.myreportlinks.com

▶**Intelligence in the War of Independence**
This CIA Web site examines the intelligence operations of the Revolutionary
War. You will learn about the involvement of George Washington, Benjamin
Franklin, and others in such operations.

Link to this Internet site from http://www.myreportlinks.com

▶**The Lafayette Collection at Cornell University**
This site contains documents that chronicle the life of Marquis de Lafayette,
the young French aristocrat who came to America to fight for American
independence. Of particular interest are those documents and other
memorabilia from the Revolutionary period.

Link to this Internet site from http://www.myreportlinks.com

▶**Little Known Facts about the American Revolutionary War**
At this Web site, you will read little known facts about the Revolutionary
War. Learn new information about key figures in the war, important events,
and more.

Link to this Internet site from http://www.myreportlinks.com

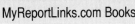
Report Links

 The Internet sites described below can be accessed at
http://www.myreportlinks.com

▶ The Paris Peace Treaty (1783)

This site holds the text of the treaty that officially ended the Revolutionary War. The agreement was signed by David Hartley for Britain and Benjamin Franklin, John Adams, and John Jay for America.

Link to this Internet site from http://www.myreportlinks.com

▶ Revolutionary Period

America's Story from America's Library, a Library of Congress Web site, provides a brief overview of the causes of the Revolutionary War.

Link to this Internet site from http://www.myreportlinks.com

▶ The Revolutionary War: A Journey towards Freedom

At this Web site you will learn about the American Revolution through a collection of images and historical documents. You will also find additional links about the American Revolution.

Link to this Internet site from http://www.myreportlinks.com

▶ Virtual Marching Tour of the American Revolution

The focus of this site is on the Philadelphia Campaign of 1777, which preceded the six-month encampment of the Continental Army at Valley Forge. Some of the battles covered include Brandywine and Germantown.

Link to this Internet site from http://www.myreportlinks.com

▶ The War for American Independence

This site features an excellent collection of Revolutionary period documents that help bring to life this critical period in American history. Among the documents are contemporary newspaper reports and three speeches by George Washington.

Link to this Internet site from http://www.myreportlinks.com

▶ 1776–1783: Diplomacy of the American Revolution

This State Department Web site tells the story of American diplomatic efforts during the Revolutionary War. Benjamin Franklin and others sought to win support for the American cause abroad.

Link to this Internet site from http://www.myreportlinks.com

Revolutionary War Facts

▶ Combatants

The Thirteen Colonies, aided by France, Holland, and a number of European noblemen.

England, aided by colonists loyal to England, hired German troops, and some American Indian tribal allies.

▶ Casualties

Note: American Revolution casualty figures vary greatly, depending on the sources consulted. Here are generally accepted battle casualties for the seven years of fighting.[1]

Total American casualties: 12,945	Total British casualties: 12,599

▶ A Brief Time Line

1765—Stamp Act arouses strong colonial opposition.

1767—Townshend Acts place unpopular duties on imports—including tea.

1773—*December 16:* Boston Tea Party.

1774—*March 31:* King George III signs first of the "Intolerable Acts."

1775—*April 19:* Battle of Lexington and Concord sheds first blood.

June 17: Battle of Bunker Hill proves that Americans can fight.

1776—*July 4:* Second Continental Congress endorses Declaration of Independence.

December 26: Washington victorious at Trenton, New Jersey.

1777—*October 17:* Americans win Battle of Saratoga.

December 17: Continental Army goes into winter quarters at Valley Forge.

1778—*February 6:* France agrees to support the United States.

1780—*May 12:* British occupy Charleston, America's worst defeat of the war.

1781—*October 19:* Cornwallis surrenders at Yorktown, Virginia.

1783—*September 3:* Treaty of Paris ends Revolutionary War.

A Shot Heard 'Round the World

British General Thomas Gage laid his plans with care. As commander of His Majesty's forces in North America, his orders were clear. King George III wanted to teach his rowdy American subjects a lesson.

The crisis had been building for months. Each new law passed by Parliament seemed to meet with more resistance. The tax on tea had aroused a special fury. On December 16, 1773, a Boston mob had boarded three British ships. Whooping and hollering, they dumped 342 chests of tea into the harbor. When the city refused to pay for the ruined tea, the Royal Navy closed the port.[1]

The fact that Parliament made rules governing the lives of the colonists, living across the Atlantic

In July 1775, the ▶ colonists sent a petition to Britain declaring loyalty to King George III, and asking him to address their complaints.

Ocean did not sit well. It might had helped if the colonists had been represented in Parliament. Although they were British subjects, that was not the case.

The Boston Tea Party pushed the colonies closer to revolution. To prepare for war, American patriots—often referred to as Minutemen because they volunteered to fight the British at a moment's notice—stockpiled guns and powder. The town of Concord, sixteen miles west of Boston, was a major collection point. Along with seizing those stores, Gage hoped to arrest Sam Adams and John Hancock. The American leaders had been staying at Lexington, a town on the Concord road. On the night of April 18, 1775, the navy ferried Colonel Francis Smith and seven hundred Redcoats (British troops wore red coats) to the mainland. Ahead of the troops, mounted patrols stopped riders who might try to sound the alarm.

Each night, patriots prowled Boston's streets watching for troop movements. When they spotted the Redcoats heading for the harbor, they lit two lanterns in the steeple of North Church. The signal sent Paul Revere and William Dawes racing to alert the countryside. As Revere later wrote, "I alarmed almost every house, till I got to Lexington."[2]

Bloodshed Begins

Revere was stopped by a British patrol near Lexington. A major held a pistol to his head. "If I did not give him true answers," Revere later wrote, "[he said] he would blow my brains out."[3] The silversmith stayed alive by telling the officer what little he knew. After being set free, Revere found Adams and Hancock and talked them into leaving Lexington. All this time, American militia soldiers had been answering the call to arms. When the Redcoats reached the village green, Captain John Parker's company was waiting. It was early in the morning of April 19, 1775.

A British officer shouted, "Lay down your arms, you damned rebels, or you are all dead men!" Parker, a doubtful legend claims, told his men, "Don't fire unless fired upon. But if they want a war, let it begin here."[4] Then, hoping to avoid bloodshed, he ordered his outnumbered troops to disperse. The Minutemen moved back but kept their muskets at the ready. Moments later a voice yelled, "Fire! By God, fire!"[5] A single pistol shot rang out, followed by a volley of musket fire. The Americans returned fire but broke and ran in the face of a bayonet

▲ This drawing illustrates Paul Revere's famous ride from Boston to Lexington in 1775.

charge. When the smoke cleared, ten militia soldiers had been wounded. Eight lay dead. The British counted one man wounded—and one horse grazed by musket balls.[6]

The Redcoats reloaded and headed for Concord. Any chance of catching the town off guard had vanished. When they arrived, the troops destroyed the few war supplies that had not been hidden. At Old North Bridge, they exchanged fire with a strong militia force. This time it was the Redcoats who were outgunned. Colonel Smith was no fool. He ordered his men to return to Boston.

▶ Lesson in Tactics

Hundreds of Minutemen converged on the retreating Redcoats. Near Meriam's Farm, Smith's nervous soldiers fired on the riflemen who had gathered there. True to their frontier training, the colonists took cover. Soon every tree, barn, and stone wall seemed to shelter a sniper. As one British soldier described the scene, it seemed "as if men came down from the clouds."[7]

The Redcoats were close to panic. The strong relief force that met them at Lexington saved the day. British artillery swept the road and the retreat continued. Angry Redcoats shot or bayoneted anyone caught with a gun in his hand. If a sniper fired from a farmhouse, they set fire to the building.

The firing stopped when the exhausted troops reached Charlestown. With British guns focused on the causeway leading to the town, the Americans backed off. Most felt content with their day's work. They had inflicted 273 casualties on the hated "Lobsterbacks," another nickname given to the British because of their bright red coats. American losses totaled ninety-three dead and wounded.[8]

▲ *A map of the Battles of Lexington and Concord. The British course of attack and retreat is in red.*

Following the encounters of Lexington and Concord, most patriots enrolled in militia units.

In trying to seize some illegal arms, Gage touched off a revolt. Militia soldiers from all over New England hurried toward Boston. By the morning of April 20, the city was surrounded. A long dispute over colonial rights had flared into open revolt.

Chapter 2 ▶

"No Taxation Without Representation"

By 1775, the colonies had outgrown their raw beginnings. As the frontier moved westward, eastern towns and cities prospered. Rich or poor, most colonists believed in the ideals of freedom and opportunity. In this new land, they said, people could rise as far as their talents allowed. However, if asked who they were, colonists were more likely to say, "I'm British," than "I'm American."

By the 1770s, many families had lived in the New World for three or four generations. Their lives were shaped by cheap land, good wages, and freedom of movement. This New World pride sometimes collided with the contempt British soldiers felt for most "Yankees." A "doodle," in the 1700s, was slang for a fool. Thus it was that the song "Yankee Doodle" was meant as an insult to all colonists, not just those from New England. When Yankee Doodle saw his first drum, the Redcoats laughed, he sang:

> There I saw a wooden keg
> With heads made out of leather.
> They knocked upon it with some sticks
> To call the folks together . . . [1]

▶ Acts of Parliament Enrage Colonists

Hurt feelings were not enough to touch off a revolt. Parliament struck the real sparks by passing acts, or laws, that ignored colonial rights. In English minds, the laws were just. To angry colonists, the measures trampled on their right to govern themselves. Two acts that added fuel to the fire were the Proclamation of 1763 and the Stamp Act.

England emerged from the French and Indian War as "owner" of much of North America. British land claims, however, ran headlong into the rights of American Indians. King George III issued the Proclamation of 1763 to keep the peace with the Ohio Valley tribes. The decree warned settlers not to venture beyond the Appalachians. This limit to settlement angered settlers who yearned for more "elbow room." Parliament added fuel to the fire by passing the Stamp Act in 1765. Without the "stamp" (which was a way of taxing documents), contracts, deeds, and even newspapers could not be issued. Colonists took to the streets to protest the new tax. Merchants joined in by boycotting British goods. The turmoil forced the repeal of the act a year later— but more trouble lay ahead.

▲ Under the Stamp Act of 1765, documents such as contracts, deeds, and even newspapers needed a special stamp.

In 1767, the Townshend Acts levied import duties on glass, lead, paints, paper—and tea. Sam Adams summed up the colonial reaction. He wrote that "what a man has honestly

File   Edit   View   Favorites   Tools   Help

Address http://www.historyplace.com/unitedstates/revolution/revgfx/bost-mass2.jpg   Go   Links

The Boston Massacre, March 5, 1770.   www.historyplace.com

Done   Internet

▲ *British soldiers killed five colonists in the Boston Massacre, which took place on March 5, 1770. Although it was not an actual massacre, it was one of the events that led to the Revolutionary War in America.*

acquired is absolutely his own, which he may freely give, but cannot be taken from him without his consent."[2] According to Parliament, the revenue was needed to pay debts incurred while protecting the colonists. Only local assemblies, Adams argued, had the right to levy taxes. James Otis reduced the issue to a five-word rallying cry: "Taxation without representation is tyranny!"[3]

A new wave of boycotts forced repeal of the Townshend Acts. Parliament kept the duty on tea to prove its right to tax the colonies. The people of Boston responded by jeering British soldiers when they appeared in the streets. On March 5, 1770, the taunting turned violent. A squad of Redcoats opened fire after a mob pelted them with snowballs. Five men died in what history calls the Boston Massacre.

▷ A "Tea Party" Causes More Friction

The colonies embarked on a collision course with the mother country. Committees of Correspondence helped plan acts of defiance. In the streets, the hotheads of the Sons of Liberty campaigned to end "British tyranny." The fires burned brighter still after the East India Company

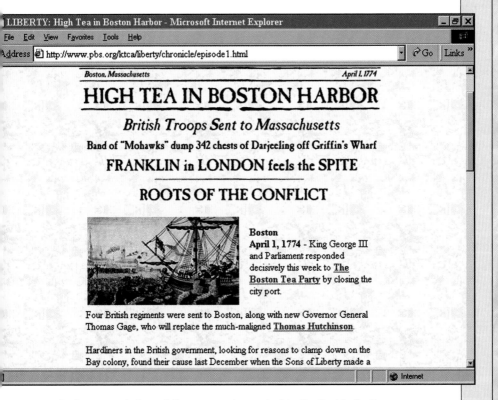

LIBERTY: High Tea in Boston Harbor - Microsoft Internet Explorer

File Edit View Favorites Tools Help

Address http://www.pbs.org/ktca/liberty/chronicle/episode1.html   Go   Links

Boston, Massachusetts   *April 1, 1774*

HIGH TEA IN BOSTON HARBOR

British Troops Sent to Massachusetts

Band of "Mohawks" dump 342 chests of Darjeeling off Griffin's Wharf

FRANKLIN in LONDON feels the SPITE

ROOTS OF THE CONFLICT

Boston
April 1, 1774 - King George III and Parliament responded decisively this week to The Boston Tea Party by closing the city port.

Four British regiments were sent to Boston, along with new Governor General Thomas Gage, who will replace the much-maligned Thomas Hutchinson.

Hardliners in the British government, looking for reasons to clamp down on the Bay colony, found their cause last December when the Sons of Liberty made a

Internet

△ *In a crusade to end the monopoly granted to the East India Company, a group of patriots dumped 342 chests of tea into the harbor on December 16, 1773.*

was granted a monopoly on tea. Rather than pay the hated Townshend duty, the colonies refused to let the tea ships dock. In Boston, three ships managed to dock but not to unload. On December 16, 1773, angry patriots boarded the ships. One by one, the protesters dumped the contents of 342 tea chests into the harbor.[4]

News of the Boston Tea Party shook England. To punish Boston, Parliament passed what Americans called the "Intolerable Acts" in 1774. Two of the laws closed the port and took away the colony's charter. Another forbade town meetings. A fourth act required that the colonists provide housing for British troops. In response, colonial leaders called the First Continental Congress. Fifty-six delegates from twelve colonies approved a tough new boycott. They also appealed to the king to right their wrongs.

King George III refused to listen. He wrote, "The New England governments are in a state of rebellion. Blows must decide whether they are to be subjects to this country or independent."[5] Patriots in Massachusetts answered by building up their militias. To supply these citizen soldiers, they stockpiled shot and powder. The shooting started when the British tried to seize the military stores kept at Concord.

On September 5, 1774, fifty-six delegates from twelve colonies attended the First Continental Congress in Philadelphia. They sought fair treatment from Great Britain rather than independence.

Chapter 3

"To Begin the World Anew"

The fighting at Lexington and Concord tipped the balance toward war. Three weeks later, on May 10, 1775, the Second Continental Congress met in Philadelphia. Delegates from twelve colonies (Georgia joined later) took up the task of governing the united colonies. Congress

▲ After Britain ignored the petition of the first Congress, the Second Continental Congress met in Philadelphia on May 10, 1775. This time, an army was organized, with George Washington as commander in chief.

chose George Washington to lead the new Continental Army. As events would prove, it was an inspired choice.

Many Americans believed their foe was Parliament, not King George III. To test that belief, Congress addressed a letter to the king. The Olive Branch Petition urged him to listen to their grievances. The headstrong king refused to read the petition when it reached London. The wayward colonies, he proclaimed, must be punished.[1]

▶ Battle of Bunker Hill

While Congress put the colonies on a war footing, militia troops laid siege to Boston, Massachusetts. On June 17,

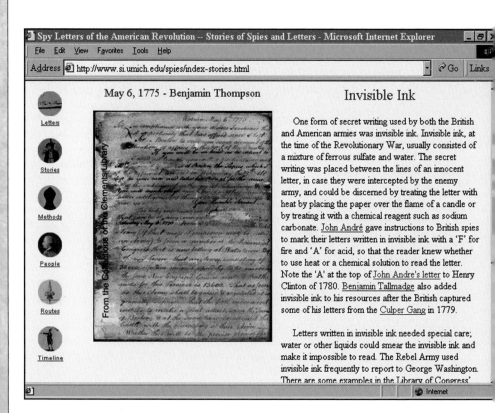

▲ *During the Revolutionary War, both the British and American armies used invisible ink to send secret messages.*

1775, the Americans tightened the noose by erecting forts on two hills that overlooked the harbor. Alarmed by the sight, the Royal Navy shelled the new trenches. General William Howe then ordered twenty-five hundred Redcoats to take the hill closest to the harbor—Breed's Hill. By a strange quirk, the battle was named for Bunker Hill, which lay behind Breed's Hill.[2]

Each Redcoat was weighed down by a 125-pound backpack. Tall grass further hampered the troops as they climbed Breed's Hill. Behind the rebel lines, Brigadier General Israel Putnam cautioned his men, "Don't fire until you see the whites of their eyes!"[3] The riflemen waited until the Redcoats had closed to thirty yards. Then they loosed a volley that shredded the British line. Howe rallied his troops for a second assault, but the results were the same. The slaughter might have gone on, but the Americans were running out of powder. The British dropped their packs, attached bayonets, and charged again. The third assault broke the American lines. The rebels withdrew after a flurry of hand-to-hand combat.

As the smoke cleared, the British counted their casualties. American gunners had accounted for 228 dead and 826 wounded—42 percent of the assault force. The heavy toll included ninety-two officers, always the favored targets of American marksmen. General Henry Clinton looked at the numbers and saw trouble ahead. "It was a dear bought victory," he said. "Another such would have ruined us."[4]

▶ Boston Victory, New York Escape

Washington arrived in Boston on July 2, 1775, to take command of the siege. He found a Continental Army that was full of fight, but short of supplies. Gunpowder had to

be smuggled in from the Dutch West Indies. In the first year, Washington wrote, there were not "more than nine cartridges to a man."[5] He also had to cope with the problem of short enlistments. Many of his militia soldiers, contracted to serve only until the end of 1775, would leave for home on December 31. The general appealed to their love of country as he urged the men to sign on for a full year.

Early in 1776, the balance tipped in the rebels' favor. Vermont's Ethan Allen and his Green Mountain Boys had seized a number of big guns after storming Fort Ticonderoga, New York. Henry Knox, the commander of American artillery, using oxcarts, dragged fifty-nine of the cannon and mortars into Washington's camp in Cambridge, Massachusetts. Knox and his men had accomplished an extraordinary engineering feat. They hauled almost sixty tons of metal three hundred miles, across the frozen Hudson River in New York and over the western hills of Massachusetts to Cambridge.[6]

Washington installed the weapons on a high point above Boston. British General Lord Howe ordered an attack, but a sudden storm forced him to call off the assault. There was nothing left to do but withdraw. On March 17, young boys bounded across Boston Neck to tell the American army that "the lobsters" were gone.[7] Howe and his army had sailed off to Nova Scotia, Canada.

The Americans had little time to celebrate. Within days, Washington was leading the army south to defend New York. Warned that Howe was coming, he set up a defense of New York City and its harbor. On June 25, the British brushed aside the defenders and landed on Staten Island. Washington and his twenty thousand soldiers found themselves facing thirty thousand Redcoats. Only half of his men were disciplined Continental soldiers. The rest were short-term militia troops. These volunteers sometimes ran when they came under heavy fire.

The Battle of Long Island nearly destroyed the Continental Army. Howe found an opening on his foe's left flank and poured men and guns into the gap. After a series of running battles, the survivors fell back to Brooklyn Heights. Howe did not want a replay of Breed's Hill. Instead of charging the strongpoint, he set up siege lines. Washington knew his army could not withstand a long siege. That night, small boats carried 9,500 American troops through the fog to safety on the island of Manhattan. Many historians view Howe's letting the Americans escape as a major missed opportunity to end the rebellion.

Thomas Paine was ▶ *an influential writer during the time of the Revolutionary War.*

▶ Declaration of Independence

The fighting around New York dragged into the fall. The Continental Army yielded ground slowly. As winter set in, Washington must have despaired at what he saw. His army had dwindled to six thousand men and he was in full retreat across New Jersey. A British report noted: "Many of the Rebels who were killed . . . were without shoes or Stockings. . . . They must suffer extremely."[8] Thomas Paine, author of *The American Crisis, 1776* and *Common Sense*, used their misery as a rallying cry. He wrote in *The American Crisis, 1776*:

> These are the times that try men's souls: . . . but he that stands it now deserves the love and thanks of man and woman. Tyranny, like Hell, is not easily conquered. Yet we have this consolation with us, that the harder the conflict, the more glorious the triumph.[9]

Paine's words were particularly powerful since he was an Englishman who had been in the colonies only two years when these two pamphlets were printed in 1776. Sales of *Common Sense* alone reached 150,000 copies, the equivalent of 15 million in modern America.[10]

The men suffered, but their spirits were high. The year had brought its share of good news. In May, France had promised to supply a million dollars worth of guns and powder. Then, on July 4, Congress had approved the Declaration of Independence. Thanks to Thomas Jefferson's inspired words, Americans knew they were fighting for "life, liberty, and the pursuit of happiness."

Chapter 4 ▶

From Low Point to Turning Point

The year 1776 was drawing to a close. The Continental Army had escaped from New York, but it was in poor shape. Food, clothing, and powder were in short supply. A wet, cold winter added to the men's woes. A lesser commander might have huddled in his tent, hoping for a miracle. George Washington created his own miracle.

The British Army, snug in winter quarters, was

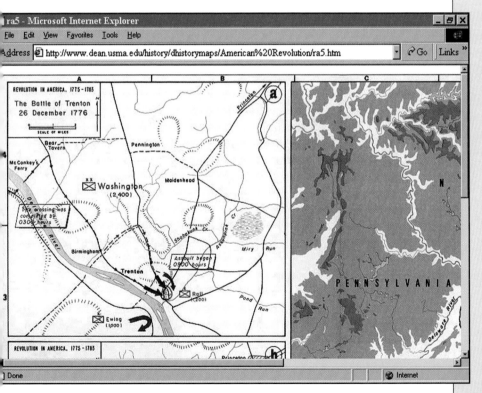

▲ This map shows how George Washington made his famous surprise crossing of the Delaware River on December 25, 1776.

enjoying the holidays. Many Tories (Americans loyal to the British) had opened their homes to General Howe and his men. Some twelve hundred hired Hessian (German mercenary) troops were stationed at Trenton, New Jersey. Colonel Johann Rall saw no need to fortify the town. To guard against an attack on his Hessians, he stationed a few patrols on the nearby roads. Rall then relaxed on Christmas Day by getting drunk.

▶ Twin Victories—Trenton and Princeton

While Rall was partying, Washington's army was marching. A fleet of forty-foot boats carried his men across the icy Delaware River. Pelted by snow and sleet, two men froze to death. Once across, the soldiers trotted the nine miles to Trenton. No one smoked or talked. An aide whispered that the men's muskets were too wet to fire. Washington replied, "Tell General Sullivan to use the bayonet. I am resolved to take Trenton."[1]

Soon after dawn, the onrushing Americans brushed Rall's patrols aside and poured into Trenton. The Hessians tumbled out of their beds and grabbed their muskets. It was too late. Rebel cannoneers raked the streets with a deadly curtain of shot. One by one the Hessian units laid down their arms. At a cost of four men wounded, the rebels had killed twenty-two Germans and 948 captives. Colonel Rall was among the dead.[2]

A few days later, near Princeton, Washington struck again. Inspired by his leadership, his troops put a strong British force to flight. The twin victories sent morale soaring. Entire units of the Continental Army voted to extend their enlistments. The Revolution was back on track.

▷ Burgoyne Meets His Match

Washington's problems were far from over. Enlistments were on the rise, but money and supplies were scarce, and the British had been spurred to greater efforts. The British plan for 1777 called for three columns to converge in upstate New York. If the strategy worked, the colonies would be cut in two. In the end, only one of the columns came close to reaching its objective.

British Major General John Burgoyne's army put on a brave show as it advanced south from Montreal. Burgoyne's troops respectfully referred to him as "Gentleman Johnny" because he treated them well.[3] After

From the Collections of the Clements Library

▲ Though he was a courageous general during much of the Revolutionary War, Benedict Arnold is better known by his reputation as a traitor.

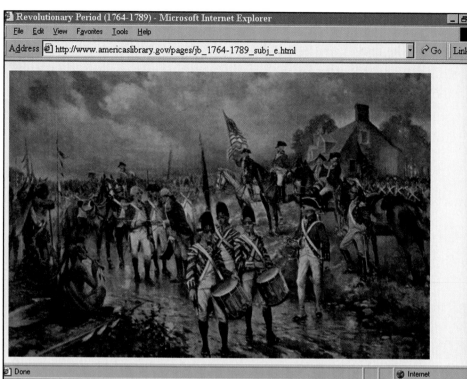

▲ *This painting depicts British Major General John Burgoyne's surrender to General Horatio Gates and Brigadier General Benedict Arnold at Saratoga in the fall of 1777.*

crushing Fort Ticonderoga, Burgoyne pressed forward. His plans called for the local Tories to provide food and horses for his seventy-two hundred men. Those hopes died as word spread that Burgoyne's Iroquois scouts, who had sided with the British against the Americans, had scalped two white women. Always fearful of "injun raids," New Yorkers turned against the British. The Redcoats trudged on, footsore and hungry.

Burgoyne ran into the Continental Army near Saratoga on September 19, 1777. The Americans, led by General Horatio Gates and Brigadier General Benedict Arnold, were dug in on Bemis Heights. Gates was as slow and careful as Arnold was quick and bold. Gates was given the nickname "Granny" because his gray hair, ruddy face, and spectacles that often slid down his nose made the fifty-year-old soldier look like an old woman.[4] Gates missed his big chance by failing to attack the British flank. Thanks to that oversight, Burgoyne held the upper hand after a day of bloody fighting. At that point, "Gentleman Johnny" drew back to wait for the column of fresh troops he thought was coming. It never arrived.

The odds had changed when the shooting started again on October 7. For once, the Redcoats were outnumbered. In a day of fierce fighting, rebel marksmen zeroed in on British officers. Gates had relieved Arnold of his command, but that did not stop the fiery general. Mounted on a white stallion, Arnold galloped into the midst of the battle. Inspired by his example, the Americans broke the British lines. Two years later, Arnold reversed the role he played at Saratoga. Driven by grudges real and imagined, he turned traitor and took up a command in the British Army.

It was this victory at Saratoga that later convinced France to send more help to the struggling American nation.

Terrible Winter, Dawn of Hope

Three days before the victory at Saratoga, Washington had stumbled at Germantown, Pennsylvania. Hampered by heavy fog, his thrust against Howe's main army quickly collapsed. As often happened, the British did not follow up their victory. Howe withdrew to the comforts of Philadelphia. Washington led his army into winter quarters at Valley Forge.

The winter of 1777 tested the army to the utmost. Men shivered in cold, drafty huts. To ease their hunger,

they ate pancakes made of flour and water. Barefoot soldiers left bloody footprints as they trudged through the snow. Typhus and smallpox swept the camp and pushed the death toll to nearly three thousand. General Nathanael Greene shared the hardships with his men. "God grant we may never be brought to such a wretched condition again!" he wrote.[5]

Washington held the army together by sheer force of will. By May, more men were joining the army. Thanks to the tireless work of a German volunteer, the men were fit and well drilled. The German, Baron Friedrich von Steuben, did not speak English, but he knew how to train raw troops. The freethinking Americans taught von Steuben a few lessons, too. He wrote, "You say to [Prussians, Austrians, or French] 'Do this,' and [they do] it. [Here] I am obliged to say, 'This is the reason why you ought to do that,' and then [the American] does it."[6]

There was more good news that spring. Out west, a tiny force led by George Rogers Clark captured three British forts. In Europe, using the victory at Saratoga to help him bargain, Ben Franklin forged an alliance with France. King Louis XIV approved a treaty in January 1778 that sent men, ships, supplies, and money to America. Spain joined the alliance a year later. Holland, long a supplier of gunpowder, came aboard late in 1780. The young American nation had reached a turning point.

◀ *Benjamin Franklin persuaded French King Louis XIV to send men, supplies, and monetary aid to America, which helped greatly in winning the Revolutionary War.*

Chapter 5 ▶

The World Turned Upside Down

Late in 1778, the southern states came under attack. Savannah, Georgia, fell to an invasion force on December 29. With the city as a base, the British pushed northward. The Continental Army pushed back. American General Benjamin Lincoln tried to retake Savannah in the summer of 1779. The Americans fought well but could not break the British defenses.

British General Henry Clinton used the victory as a springboard. Backed up by the Royal Navy, his troops besieged Charleston, South Carolina. The city's fiery ordeal began in April 1780 with a barrage of red-hot shot—cannon balls heated glowing red to set fire to their target. Day by day the Redcoats tightened their siege lines. Rather than see the city burned to the ground, the Americans gave up. At a cost of just 265 casualties, Clinton netted over four thousand captives and a huge store of supplies. Historians rank the loss of Charleston as America's worst defeat of the war. It rivaled the British defeat at Saratoga.[1]

▶ A New Kind of War

In the weeks that followed, British troops rampaged through the South. A desperate Congress sent Horatio Gates to turn the tide. Gates could not repeat his big win at Saratoga. Nothing went right when he met the British at Camden, South Carolina, in August. A well-timed cavalry charge broke his line and forced Gates to flee. Congress replaced him with Nathanael Greene.

http://www.historyplace.com/unitedstates/revolution/revgfx/gates.jpg - Microsoft Internet Explorer

File Edit View Favorites Tools Help

Address http://www.historyplace.com/unitedstates/revolution/revgfx/gates.jpg Go Links

Done Internet

▲ *In August 1780, British troops under General Charles Cornwallis almost destroyed Horatio Gates's army at Camden, South Carolina. General Nathanael Greene replaced Gates (shown here) in December 1780.*

One of Greene's first moves was to turn Colonel Daniel Morgan loose in South Carolina. The tactic paid off at the Battle of Cowpens on January 17, 1781. Outnumbered and pinned against a nearby river, Morgan fought a brilliant battle. He utilized his little army well— South Carolina militia, Virginia riflemen, cavalry, and experienced Continentals. As the British charged, Morgan's first two lines of troops each fired two sharp volleys and moved back. The Redcoats kept coming, only to run into a third line of marksmen. These troops also fired and pulled back. The elated British rushed forward— and stumbled into a trap. Morgan rallied his men, who fixed bayonets and charged the British left flank. At the same time, the American cavalry swept in on the right flank. The sudden pincerlike movement routed the Redcoats.[2]

General Charles Cornwallis chased Greene and Morgan into North Carolina. In March 1781, Greene challenged his pursuer at Guilford Court House. The fighting surged back and forth, with the two armies locked in hand-to-hand combat. Fearing that the battle was lost, Cornwallis ordered his gunners to sweep the field with grapeshot. The deadly cannon pellets mowed down friend and foe alike. The Americans withdrew, leaving the field to Cornwallis.[3]

Weakened by heavy losses, Cornwallis withdrew northward. Greene regrouped and went on to fight the battles that freed the lower South. With their troops on the defensive, the British called on the Royal Navy to tip the balance.

▶ War at Sea

Americans were a seafaring people, but they had to build a navy from scratch. As a result, the Royal Navy far outnumbered the Continental Navy. Adding to the imbalance, most American ships started life as merchantmen (ships used for commerce). In combat, British men-of-war often outgunned these slow-sailing warships.

Captain John Paul Jones and his ship, the *Bonhomme Richard,* showed that skill and daring could even the odds. In September 1779, Jones pitted his ex-merchant ship against HMS *Serapis.* In a running battle, the ships exchanged broadsides with British guns, inflicting disastrous damage to the *Bonhomme Richard.* British gunners silenced the *Richard's* cannon one by one. As the ships

closed to close quarters, the *Serapis* offered the *Richard* a chance to surrender. Jones shouted back, "I have not yet begun to fight!"[4]

Inspired by their captain, the Americans fought on with grenades and muskets. Night fell, and still the battle raged. At last, with the *Serapis'* mast about to fall, the British captain hauled down his flag. The Americans took control of the *Serapis*. The gallant *Richard* sank as the Americans sailed away in the captured frigate.

The Continental Navy captured or sank nearly two hundred British ships during the war. A fleet of swift privateers commissioned by Congress did much of the damage. A privateer is a privately owned armed vessel whose owners are commissioned by a nation to carry on naval warfare. Such naval commissions or authorizations are called letters of marque or reprisal. The practice, common in the 1700s, paid off. Privateers seized more than three thousand British merchant ships. The risks, as well as the payoffs, were great. Half of the privateers that put to sea never returned.[5]

▶ Caught in a Vise

The Royal Navy had its hands full after France declared war against Great Britain. In a struggle that ranged the world's seas, British ships won more than their share of battles. Only in North America did French sea power turn a deadlock into a triumph.

The final battle began quietly. After the long southern campaign, Cornwallis headed north to Yorktown, Virginia. Along with the city's strong defenses, Cornwallis had Chesapeake Bay at his back. The navy would sail in and rescue him if the rebels tried to spring a trap.

The news from Yorktown reached Washington while he was planning an attack on New York. As he considered his options, the French told him that their fleet would support a thrust against Yorktown. Washington swiftly shifted his forces southward.

French Admiral de Grasse quickly closed Cornwallis's escape hatch. Five days later, the British fleet sailed in to challenge the French blockade of Yorktown. In the battle that followed, de Grasse outsailed his British opponent. The British ships were forced to limp away, leaving Cornwallis with no hope of rescue. General George Weedon bragged, "We have got [Cornwallis] . . . in a pudding bag."[6]

Cornwallis did his best to break out of the vise. He launched attack after attack, but the Americans held fast. Jean Baptiste Rochambeau, a French general, supported the Americans with a large contingent of French soldiers and marines. To escape the rain of shells, Cornwallis mapped out a route across the York River. A sudden storm spoiled that plan. With all hope gone, Cornwallis surrendered his eight thousand troops. His sullen soldiers surrendered on October 19. Legend says that the band picked that moment to strike up a popular tune. The fitting title: "The World Turned Upside Down."[7]

French and American ▶ troops surrounded General Charles Cornwallis at Yorktown, Virginia, on October 19, 1781. His surrender was critical to the American triumph.

The Treaty of Paris

The news from Yorktown set off a grand celebration. Patriots danced around bonfires, shot off rockets, and feasted on roast oxen. Carried by ship, the word did not reach London until weeks later. The British prime minister, Lord North, reacted as though he had "taken a [musket] ball in the breast."[1]

The cheers soon faded. George Washington warned his countrymen not to let down their guard. " . . . A relaxation in the prosecution of the war," he wrote, might well " . . . prolong the calamities of it."[2] As usual, the general was correct. The British held New York, Charleston, and other key cities. Tories joined with American Indians in an attack on a frontier settlement. In South Carolina, the army fought one last skirmish with British troops.

▶ Treaty of Paris

The Royal Navy evened the score by defeating Admiral de Grasse and his fleet in April 1782 in the Battle of Santo Domingo. With national pride restored, Parliament voted to make peace. General Guy Carleton withdrew his forces from Savannah and Charleston. A peace commission held its first sessions in Paris that summer. By late fall, England and the United States had reached an agreement. England then hammered out a peace treaty with France, Spain, and Holland. On September 3, 1783, the delegates signed the Treaty of Paris. The Revolutionary War was over.

The peace treaty addressed the war's major issues. First, England granted the former colonies their independence. A second section guaranteed free ship passage on the Mississippi River to the five nations that signed the treaty. A third section handed Florida back to Spain and the African colony of Senegal to France. The treaty also protected America's fishing rights off Newfoundland.

New Challenges for the Young Nation

With the war over, the United States faced new tests. One task was to repair war damage. New York, Charleston, and

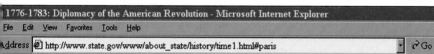

Treaty of Paris, 1783

In April 1782 Benjamin Franklin rejected informal peace feelers from Great Britain for a settlement that would provide the thirteen states with some measure of autonomy within the British empire. Franklin insisted on British recognition of American independence and refused to consider a peace separate from France, America's staunch ally. Franklin did agree to negotiations with the British for an end to the war. Joined by peace commissioners John Adams and John Jay, Franklin engaged the British in formal negotiations beginning on September 27, 1782. Although Franklin demanded the cessation of Canada to an independent America, he knew that the British Government of Lord Shelburne, opposed to American independence, was unprepared to accept that offer. Two months of hard bargaining resulted in a preliminary articles of peace in which the British accepted American independence and boundaries-- a bitter pill to George III--resolved the difficult issues of fishing rights on the Newfoundland banks and prewar debts owed British creditors, promised restitution of property lost during the war by Americans loyal to the British cause, and provided for the evacuation of British forces from the thirteen states. The preliminary articles signed in Paris on November 30, 1782, were only effective when a similar treaty was signed by Britain and France, which French Foreign Minister Vergennes quickly negotiated. France signed preliminary articles of peace with Great Britain on January 20, 1783, which were followed by a formal peace of Paris signed on September 3, 1783. The illustration above, a copy of a sketch by the studio of Benjamin West, shows the American negotiators of the Peace of Paris. The sketch remains incomplete because British negotiators chose not to sit for their half of the portrait; it served as a powerful symbol of the division between Great Britain and its former American colonies.

The delegates signed the Treaty of Paris on September 3, 1783, thus granting the American colonies their independence and officially ending the Revolutionary War.

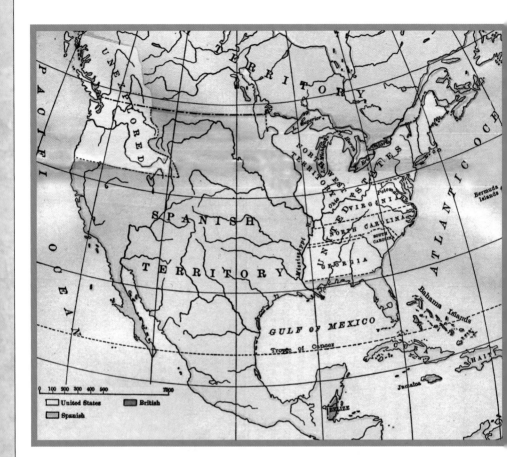

▲ *The Treaty of Paris of 1783 gave the Americans much of the land that makes up the present-day United States east of the Mississippi River.*

other cities lay half in ruins. In the countryside, weeds choked abandoned fields. Americans put down their guns and went to work.

The second task was to safeguard democracy. Some people would have preferred rule by a monarch or a dictator. Soon after Yorktown, Colonel Lewis Nicola urged Washington to proclaim himself king. Washington had no wish to wear a crown. He told Nicola to "banish those thoughts from your mind."[3] The general acted just as firmly when the army, long unpaid, seethed with talk of taking over the government. On March 12, 1783, Washington called an assembly of his fellow officers in Newburgh, New York. In his speech, he promised that the overdue money would be paid. Then, as he tried to read a letter to them, he stopped and fumbled for his glasses. "Gentlemen," he said, "you will permit me to put on my spectacles, for I have not only grown gray but almost blind in the service of my country." The words struck home. Battle-hardened men wept as they voted to wait for Congress to find the money to pay them.[4] Washington's stirring words had headed off a possible revolt by his own officers.

Writing a New Constitution

The Articles of Confederation had carried the United States through the postwar years. Now, with peace at hand, the young and weak central government was in trouble. The states argued over boundaries, tariffs, and court cases. Money was so scarce that commerce was coming to a standstill. As Alexander Hamilton put it, "The republic is sick and wants powerful remedies."[5]

The quest for a cure led to the Constitutional Convention of 1787. The states sent their best and brightest to Philadelphia that summer. With Washington presiding, the members of the Convention worked to save the republic. They had to write a constitution that would describe the nature, functions, and limits of the government of the new republic known as the United States of America.

States' rights had to be balanced against the need to create a strong central government. After much debate, the Constitution of the United States was signed, and a new

▲ After serving as commander in chief during the Revolutionary War, George Washington became the first president of the United States of America.

federal government was given the power to levy taxes, regulate commerce, and provide for the common defense. The framers also installed a system of federal government with three branches, or divisions: legislative (Congress), executive (the president and his cabinet), and judicial (the Supreme Court). This structure of government established a series of checks and balances among the three branches to safeguard the rights of American citizens.

In September 1787, the framers sent the Constitution to the states to be voted upon. By May 1788, eleven states had ratified the Constitution. North Carolina came aboard a year later, Rhode Island in 1790. As Benjamin Rush wrote, the Constitution "makes a man both willing to live and to die. To live, because it opens to him fair prospects of great public and private happiness. To die, because it ensures peace, order, safety and prosperity to his children."[6]

On April 30, 1789, Washington took the oath of office as the nation's first president. The United States of America was ready to reap the fruits of its long fight for independence.

Chapter Notes

Revolutionary War Facts

1. Sons of the Revolution in California, "Major Battles and Skirmishes of the American Revolution: 1775–1777," n.d., <http://www.walika.com/sr/Battles1775–77a.htm> (July 27, 2001); "Major Battles and Skirmishes of the American Revolution: 1778–1781,"n.d., <http://www.walika.com/sr/Battles1778–81a.htm> (July 27, 2001).

Chapter 1. A Shot Heard 'Round the World

1. Richard B. Morris, ed., *The New World, Vol. 1: Prehistory to 1774* (New York: Time Inc., 1963), p. 154.

2. Paul Revere, "Lanterns in the North Church Steeple," in David Colbert, ed., *Eyewitness to America* (New York: Vintage Books, 1998), p. 80.

3. Ibid., p. 81.

4. "13 Things You Never Knew About the American Revolution," *The American Revolution Home Page*, n.d., <http://webpages.homestead.com/revwar/files/THINGS.htm> (July 25, 2001).

5. Richard B. Morris, ed., *The Making of a Nation*, Vol. 2: 1775–1789 (New York: Time Inc., 1963), p. 8.

6. James L. Stokesbury, *A Short History of the American Revolution* (New York: William Morrow and Co., 1991), p. 15.

7. Colonel R. Ernest Dupuy and Colonel Trevor N. Dupuy, *An Outline History of the American Revolution* (New York: Harper & Row, Publishers, 1975), p. 21.

8. Morris, *Making of a Nation*, p. 8.

Chapter 2. "No Taxation Without Representation"

1. Harry Alonzo, ed., "Circular letter to the Colonial Legislatures," *The Writing of Samual Adams*, 1987, <http://press-pubs.uchicago.edu/founders/documents/v1ch17s13.html> (March 7, 2002).

2. Theodore Draper, *A Struggle for Power: The American Revolution* (New York: Vintage Books, 1996), p. 316.

3. Robert Leckie, *The World Turned Upside Down: the Story of the American Revolution* (New York: G.P. Putnam's Sons, 1973), p. 16.

4. Richard B. Morris, ed., *The New World, Vol. 1: Prehistory to 1774* (New York: Time Inc., 1963), p. 154.

5. Ibid., p. 155.

Chapter 3. "To Begin the World Anew"

1. Richard B. Morris, ed., *The Making of a Nation*, Vol. 2: 1775–1789 (New York: Time Inc., 1963), p. 34.

2. "The Battle of Bunker Hill," *The American Revolution Home Page*, n.d., <http://webpages.homestead.com/revwar/files /Bunker.htm> (July 10, 2001).

3. Colonel R. Ernest Dupuy and Colonel Trevor N. Dupuy, *An Outline History of the American Revolution* (New York: Harper & Row, Publishers, 1975), p. 24.

4. Don Higginbotham, "The Battle of Bunker Hill," *The American Revolution Home Page, 1998–1999*, <http://www.irqpa .org/1phs/1948/4th/BUNKER.HTM> (March 13, 2002).

5. Barbara Tuchman, *The First Salute* (New York: Alfred A. Knopf, 1988), p. 7.

6. Thomas Fleming, *Liberty!: The American Revolution* (New York: Viking Penguin, 1997), p. 164.

7. Ibid., p. 166.

8. Morris, p. 15.

9. "Conflict and Resolution, 1775 to 1776," *The History Place*, n.d., <http://historyplace.com/unitedstates/revolution/ revwar-75.htm> (March 7, 2002).

10. Fleming, p. 159.

Chapter 4. From Low Point to Turning Point

1. "Battles . . . Trenton," *The American Revolution Home Page*, n.d., <http://webpages.homestead.com/revwar/files/Battles.htm> (July 6, 2001).

2. Colonel R. Ernest Dupuy and Colonel Trevor N. Dupuy, *An Outline History of the American Revolution* (New York: Harper & Row, Publishers, 1975), p. 72.

3. Thomas Fleming, *Liberty!: The American Revolution* (New York: Viking Penguin, 1997), p. 239.

4. Ibid., p. 245.

5. Richard B. Morris, ed., *The Making of a Nation*, Vol. 2: 1775–1789 (New York: Time Inc., 1963), p. 64.

6. Dupuy and Dupuy, p. 121.

Chapter 5. The World Turned Upside Down

1. James L. Stokesbury, *A Short History of the American Revolution* (New York: William Morrow and Co., 1991), p. 231.

2. Ibid., p. 237.

3. Richard B. Morris, ed., *The Making of a Nation, Vol. 2: 1775–1789* (New York: Time Inc., 1963), p. 84.

4. Colonel R. Ernest Dupuy and Colonel Trevor N. Dupuy, *An Outline History of the American Revolution* (New York: Harper & Row, Publishers, 1975), p. 144.

5. Stokesbury, p. 169.

6. Morris, p. 86.

7. Webb Garrison, *Sidelights on the American Revolution* (Nashville, Tenn.: Abingdon Press, 1974), p. 155.

Chapter 6. The Treaty of Paris

1. Milton Meltzer, *The American Revolutionaries: A History in Their Own Words, 1750–1800* (New York: Thomas Crowell, 1987), p. 178.

2. "The Treaty of Paris," *The American Revolution Home Page*, n.d., <http://webpages.homestead.com/revwar/files/Treaty.htm> (July 10, 2001).

3. John R. Alden, *George Washington: A Biography* (Baton Rouge: Louisiana State University Press, 1984), p. 205.

4. George L. Marshall, Jr., "The Rise and Fall of the Newburgh Conspiracy," *Archiving Early America*, n.d., <http://earlyamerica.com/review/fall97/wshngton.html> (July 28, 2001).

5. Richard B. Morris, ed., *The Making of a Nation, Vol. 2: 1775–1789* (New York: Time Inc., 1963), p. 104.

6. Ibid., p. 137.

Further Reading

Aronson, Virginia. *Ethan Allan.* Broomall, Pa.: Chelsea House Publishers, 2001.

Cox, Clinton. *Come All You Brave Soldiers: Blacks in the Revolutionary War.* New York: Scholastic, Inc., 1999.

Greene, Meg. *Nathanael Greene.* Broomall, Pa.: Chelsea House Publishers, 2001.

Grote, JoAnn A. *Lafayette.* Broomall, Pa.: Chelsea House Publishers, 2001.

Kent, Deborah. *The American Revolution: "Give Me Liberty, or Give Me Death!"* Hillside, N.J.: Enslow Publishers, Inc., 1994.

McCarthy, Pat. *Thomas Paine: Revolutionary Patriot and Writer.* Berkeley Heights, N.J.: Enslow Publishers, Inc., 2001.

Masoff, Joy. *American Revolution, 1700–1800.* New York: Scholastic, Inc., 2000.

Meltzer, Milton. *The American Revolutionaries: A History in Their Own Words, 1750–1800.* New York: Thomas Y. Crowell, 1987.

Nardo, Don. *The American Revolution.* San Diego, Calif.: Greenhaven Press, Inc., 2002.

Sanford, William R. and Carl R. Green. *The Revolutionary War Soldier at Saratoga.* Mankato, Minn.: Capstone Press, 1991.

Washington, George and Dorothy Twohig, ed. *George Washington's Diaries: An Abridgment.* Charlottesville, Va.: University Press of Virginia, 1999.

Wood, W. J. *Battles of the Revolutionary War, 1775–1781.* Chapel Hill, N.C.: Algonquin Books of Chapel Hill, 1990.